' Information Service
k/libraries
'61511

KT-429-156

Rainforest Food Chains

Emma Lynch

A L I S
1809231

www.heinemann.co.uk/library
Visit our website to find out more information about Heinemann Library books.

To order:
 Phone 44 (0) 1865 888066
 Send a fax to 44 (0) 1865 314091
 Visit the Heinemann Bookshop at www.heinemann.co.uk/library to browse our catalogue and order online.

First published in Great Britain by Heinemann Library, Halley Court, Jordan Hill, Oxford OX2 8EJ, part of Harcourt Education. Heinemann is a registered trademark of Harcourt Education Ltd.

© Harcourt Education Ltd 2005
First published in paperback in 2006
The moral right of the proprietor has been asserted.

All rights reserved. No part of this publication may be reproduced, stored in a retrieval system, or transmitted in any form or by any means, electronic, mechanical, photocopying, recording, or otherwise, without either the prior written permission of the Publishers or a licence permitting restricted copying in the United Kingdom issued by the Copyright Licensing Agency Ltd, 90 Tottenham Court Road, London W1T 4LP (www.cla.co.uk).

Editorial: Sarah Eason and Kathy Peltan
Design: Jo Hinton-Malivoire and AMR
Illustration: Words and Publications
Picture Research: Ruth Blair and Ginny Stroud-Lewis
Production: Camilla Smith

Originated by Ambassador Litho Ltd.
Printed in China by WKT Company Limited.

The paper used to print this book comes from sustainable resources.

ISBN 0431 11901 5 (hardback)
08 07 06 05
10 9 8 7 6 5 4 3 2

ISBN 0431 11908 2 (paperback)
09 08 07 06
10 9 8 7 6 5 4 3 2 1

British Library Cataloguing in Publication Data
Lynch, Emma
Food Chains: Rainforests
577.3'416

A full catalogue record for this book is available from the British Library.

Lynch, Emma
Rainforest food chains / Emma Lynch
J577.
341
1809231

Acknowledgements
The Publishers would like to thank the following for permission to reproduce photographs: a-z botanical pp. 5 (Bjorn Svensson), 8 (Bjorn Svensson), 17, 24; Corbis pp. 13 Kevin Schafer, 18 (Michael & Patricia Fogden), 22 (Kennan Ward), 14 (David A. Northcott); FLPA pp. 15 (Terry Whittaker), 19 (Arne Hodalic); NHPA pp. 25, (Natalie Fobes), 26 (John Shaw), 27 (M. Smirnoff), Heather Angel/Natural Visions pp. 20, 21; Nature Picture Library pp. 7, 9, 10, 11 (Staffan Widstrand); Oxford Scientific Films pp. 6, 16 (Peter Oxford), 16 (Doug Allan); NHPA p. 23.

Cover photograph of a toucan eating fruit reproduced with permission of Bruce Coleman/ Staffan Widstrand.

The Publishers would like to thank Michael Scott for his assistance in the preparation of this book.

Disclaimer
All Internet addresses (URLs) given in this book were valid at the time of going to press. However, due to the dynamic nature of the Internet, some addresses may have changed, or sites may have changed or ceased to exist since publication. While the author and Publishers regret any inconvenience this may cause readers, no responsibility for any such changes can be accepted by either the author or the Publishers.

Every effort has been made to contact copyright holders of any material reproduced in this book. Any omissions will be rectified in subsequent printings if notice is given to the Publishers.

Contents

What is a rainforest food web? 4

What is a rainforest food chain? 6

Which producers live in rainforests? 11

Which primary consumers live in rainforests? 13

Which secondary consumers live in rainforests? 15

Which decomposers live in rainforests? 17

How are rainforest food chains different in different places? 19

What happens to a food web when a food chain breaks down? 22

How can we protect rainforest food chains? 25

Where are the world's main rainforests? 28

Glossary 30

Find out more 31

Index 32

Words written in bold, **like this**, are explained in the Glossary.

What is a rainforest food web?

All living things, including plants, **fungi**, animals (and humans) are **organisms**. Organisms are eaten by other organisms. Small animals are eaten by bigger animals. These animals get eaten by even larger animals. When large animals die they get eaten by tiny insects, maggots and **bacteria**. Even mighty trees die and rot and are eaten by beetles, grubs and fungi. If you draw lines between each of the animals, showing who eats who, you create a diagram called a food web. It looks like a tangled spider's web!

In rainforests, just as in all **habitats**, the organisms that live there are part of a food web. In food web diagrams, the arrow leads from the food to the animal that eats it, from **prey** to **predator**.

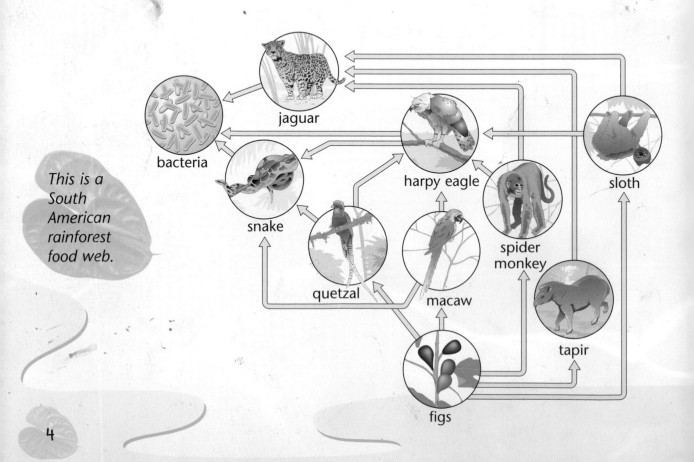

This is a South American rainforest food web.

jaguar

bacteria

snake

harpy eagle

sloth

quetzal

macaw

spider monkey

tapir

figs

What are rainforest habitats like?

This book looks at the food web and food chains of rainforest habitats. Rainforests are found in places with a **tropical climate**, usually near the **equator**. The climate is hot, and there is heavy rainfall all through the year.

Particular plants and animals live in the rainforest because they are especially suited or **adapted** to life there, and because the plants or animals that they feed on live there. Some, like mosses and jaguars, live on the forest floor. Plants such as vines and palms live in the dark **understorey**. Animals such as monkeys and sloths live in the trees. Birds such as the harpy eagle fly through the treetops, called the **canopy** level, or above the forest, looking for animals to catch and eat.

This rainforest habitat is in the Caribbean island of Grenada.

What is a rainforest food chain?

A food web looks quite complex but it is actually made up of lots of much simpler food chains. These food chains show the way some of the animals in a food web feed on each other. The arrows in the chain show the movement of food and **energy** from plants to animals as they feed on each other. More than half of the world's animal and plant **species** live in **tropical** rainforests, so the rainforest food web is made up of millions of food chains.

An **organism** can be part of more than one food chain in a food web. Most animals eat more than one type of food, because that gives them a better chance of survival than if they just depend on one food source. They will also probably be eaten by more than one kind of animal!

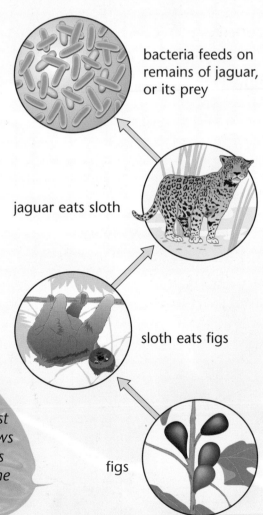

bacteria feeds on remains of jaguar, or its prey

jaguar eats sloth

sloth eats figs

figs

This is a South American rainforest food chain. It shows how energy passes from one link in the chain to another.

Starting the chain

Most food chains start with the energy that comes from the Sun. Plants take up water from the soil through their roots and **carbon dioxide** from the air through their leaves. Their leaves also trap the energy from sunlight and use this to convert the water and carbon dioxide into sugary food. This process is called **photosynthesis**. Plants use this food, along with **nutrients** from the soil, to grow.

Every part of a growing plant can become food for other organisms in the **habitat**. They can eat the plant's roots, shoots, leaves, nuts, fruit, bark – or even the rotten plant when it has died. Animals cannot make their own food, so they eat the plants to get energy. Plant-eating animals may be eaten by other bigger animals, which get energy from them. In this way the energy flows through the food chain and through the habitat.

*Rainforest trees spread a dense **canopy** of leaves to catch as much of the Sun's light as they can.*

Making the chain

Plants are called **producers**, because they trap the Sun's energy and produce food for themselves and other animals. Producers provide food for the plant-eating animals we call **herbivores**. In food chains we call these herbivores **primary consumers**. Primary consumers are often food for other animals we call **carnivores**. In food chains we call these carnivores **secondary consumers**. Secondary consumers catch and eat primary consumers, and they may also eat other smaller secondary consumers.

Primary consumers that eat both plants and other animals are called **omnivores**. Omnivores can also be secondary consumers.

Squirrel monkeys are omnivores. They eat mainly flowers, fruits and seeds, but also insects and other small animals.

More links in the chain

Food chains usually start with producers, then go on to primary consumers and secondary consumers. But the chain does not end there. All organisms eventually die. When they die, animals called **scavengers**, such as worms and maggots, eat their bodies. **Decomposers**, such as **bacteria** and **fungi** then eat or break down any dead remains that are left. They also eat or break down rotting trees and plants. The waste from these decomposers sinks into the soil or riverbed, where some of it becomes nutrients that can be **absorbed** by plant roots. In this way the chain begins again.

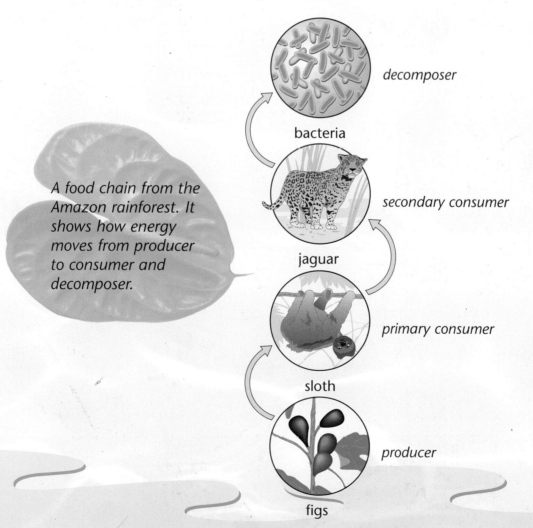

A food chain from the Amazon rainforest. It shows how energy moves from producer to consumer and decomposer.

decomposer

bacteria

secondary consumer

jaguar

primary consumer

sloth

producer

figs

Breaking the chain

If some of the organisms in a food web die out, it may be disastrous for other animals in the web. Sometimes natural events can damage a food web, but more often in the case of rainforests, human activity is the biggest threat. Rainforests are destroyed either for timber or to make space for cattle or industry. This has a deadly impact on the animals of the rainforest, which lose their food supplies, habitat and shelter. **Pollution** from **mining** and industry can also cause breaks in rainforest food chains and in natural cycles, with terrible results.

Forest fires can sometimes be started by lightning strikes. Such natural events disrupt food webs by destroying large areas of rainforest.

Which producers live in rainforests?

Plants are **producers** and they are at the start of most rainforest food chains. There are many producers in a rainforest **habitat**. There are plants growing on the forest floor, such as shrubs and moss. Ferns, vines, palms and creepers grow in the **understorey**, as they do not need much light to grow. They provide food and shelter for insects, birds and small **rodents**. Up in the trees, leaves, bark, fruit and nuts provide food for monkeys, birds and insects. Other plants called **epiphytes** grow on the trees. They get their **nutrients** from air, rainwater and waste material on the branches they grow on.

decomposer
bacteria

secondary consumer
jaguar

primary consumer
sloth

producer
figs

Mosses and ferns cover the floor of the rainforest and the lower parts of the trees.

Many rainforest producers also produce brightly coloured flowers and fruit that grow high up at the **canopy** level. These are an important food for the parrots and butterflies that inhabit this part of the rainforest. The insects and birds **pollinate** the flowers.

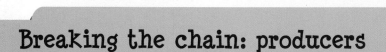

These fruits of the black bean plant are eaten by the insects and birds that live in the canopy of the Australian rainforest.

Breaking the chain: producers

Green plants are crucial to rainforest food chains, but they are in grave danger. It is thought that over 80,000 hectares (200,000 acres) of rainforest are burned down every day around the world – that's 60 hectares (150 acres) of trees, with all the plant life that grows on and around them, lost every minute. Without those trees and plants, there is no food and shelter for the animals that depend on them. Even the soil the trees grow in soon becomes poor. Thousands of **species** of are at risk of **extinction**.

Which primary consumers live in rainforests?

Primary consumers in the rainforest can be small or large animals that live on the forest floor and up in the trees. They feed on the rich plant life of the forest, from the fruit, flowers and leaves of the trees, to the shrubs and moss that grow at ground level.

On the Amazon forest floor, insects such as leaf-cutter ants and beetles forage through the **leaf litter**, nibbling the leaves and **fungi**. Ground **rodents** such as agoutis and pacas scuttle through the forest at night, searching for plants to eat.

Larger primary consumers include the tapir, a **nocturnal** animal that looks like a pig with a long, bendy nose. Tapirs spend the day in the undergrowth then come out at night to feed on leaves and fruit. They often cover themselves in a layer of mud, as a protection from insect bites!

bacteria — decomposer

jaguar — secondary consumer

sloth — primary consumer

figs — producer

*A Baird's tapir munching on Amazon rainforest plants. There are four **species** of tapir, and all of them are now **endangered**.*

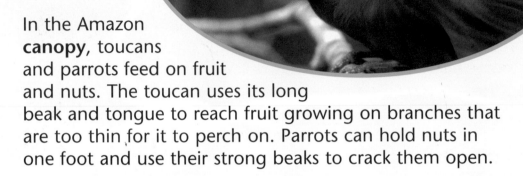

This male great bird of paradise is from Papua New Guinea, in south-eastern Asia. There are over 40 species of birds of paradise. Most eat a mixture of insects and fruit.

In the Amazon **canopy**, toucans and parrots feed on fruit and nuts. The toucan uses its long beak and tongue to reach fruit growing on branches that are too thin for it to perch on. Parrots can hold nuts in one foot and use their strong beaks to crack them open.

Fruit bats sleep all day then come out at night to feed on fruit, **nectar** and **pollen**. Brightly-coloured butterflies flutter through the trees, feeding on the nectar in their flowers. Hummingbirds are also nectar feeders. Their wings move so fast that they are a blur. They hover in mid-air as they dip their long bills into flowers.

The three-toed sloth is a strange and slow-moving animal that hangs from the branches of trees (even when it is asleep) and grinds leaves very slowly in its teeth. Its hairy coat is green from the mosses and tiny plants that grow on it. It blends in with the leaves, and moves so slowly it is difficult for **predators** to spot it. If a jaguar sees a sloth it will try to climb up and catch it.

Which secondary consumers live in rainforests?

Secondary consumers can be **carnivores** or **omnivores**. A carnivore's food is rich in **nutrients** but is not always easy to catch, so **predators** must put a lot of **energy** into hunting their **prey**. Big cats like the jaguar, ocelot and margay are rainforest predators.

Jaguars are the largest secondary consumers in the Amazon rainforest. They prowl around the forest floor and will eat any unwary animal they find. Jaguars like to eat tapir, but they also eat monkeys, water birds, caiman and tortoises.

The largest flying predator in the Amazon rainforest is the huge harpy eagle. Harpy eagles soar over the treetops then swoop down to snatch prey with their strong talons (claws). They also eat other birds, monkeys and sloths.

decomposer
bacteria

secondary consumer
jaguar

primary consumer
sloth

producer
figs

Jaguars are good swimmers and will even follow their prey into water.

The Giant Anaconda is one of the largest snakes in the world. It lives along the banks of the Amazon River and preys on **mammals** and birds that go there to drink. It drags them under the water, then kills and swallows them. Anacondas can climb as well as swim and use the rainforest trees to hide from their prey.

Sometimes plants can be predators! There are some rainforest plants, such as the pitcher plant, that trap small insects and spiders. They attract the insects into their cup-shaped leaves by leaving **nectar** at the top of the 'cup'. The insect falls into the plant, then cannot get out. The plant **absorbs** the nutrients from the insect's body to help it grow.

The deep flower of this Madagascar pitcher plant is a deadly trap for unwary insects.

Omnivores hunt for prey, but they also eat many kinds of plants. In the Australian rainforest, the bandicoot feeds on fruits, or digs its snout and claws into the ground to find insects to eat. It also eats small mammals.

Which decomposers live in rainforests?

Every acre of rainforest is filled with about two tonnes (about 2 tons) of plant and animal waste every year. If this dead matter and waste just stayed on the ground, air and water could not get through to the tree roots and **nutrients** would not be recycled for plants to **absorb**. However, the **decomposers** and **scavengers** on the rainforest floor help to recycle all the waste matter. When plants and animals die, decomposers break down the decaying matter into simpler substances, such as **carbon dioxide** and water.

In the rainforest, this recycling happens faster than anywhere else on Earth, because of the high temperature and **humidity**. The main rainforest decomposers are tiny **micro-organisms**, such as **bacteria**, and **fungi**.

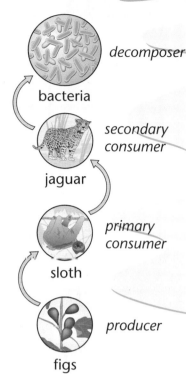

decomposer

bacteria

secondary consumer

jaguar

primary consumer

sloth

producer

figs

These bracket fungi are growing on a tree stump in Costa Rica. The 'brackets' are only a small part of the fungus. A network of tiny tubes spreads deep inside the wood.

When a tree falls to the rainforest floor it is soon covered with insects and fungi which eat the wood and bark. Termites are particularly helpful scavengers in the rainforest, as they are extremely efficient wood eaters. The holes and tunnels that termites dig provide a route for decomposers such as fungi to get deep into the wood. The insects and decomposers work so well that a dead branch in the rainforest disappears completely in just a week or two.

When an animal dies in the rainforest, it is quickly decomposed by fungi and bacteria, with the help of earthworms. The animal's body rots and releases nutrients. These sink into the soil of the rainforest floor and are absorbed by the plants, enabling them to start their life processes again.

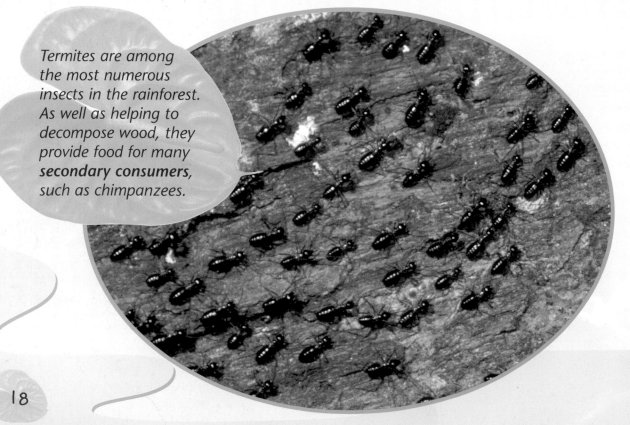

Termites are among the most numerous insects in the rainforest. As well as helping to decompose wood, they provide food for many secondary consumers, such as chimpanzees.

How are rainforest food chains different in different places?

There are rainforests all over the world – in South America, southeastern Asia, Australia and central Africa. Although these rainforests share similar **climates** and dense forests, the food chains can be very different. Food chains depend on the location of the rainforest and which animals have evolved or settled there. Human activity also affects the food chains.

The Australian rainforest is small but it is home to some remarkable animals, such as this cassowary bird.

The Amazon rainforest

The Amazon rainforest is the largest in the world. It runs through Central and South America and covers approximately 4.1 million square kilometres (1.6 million square miles) in Brazil alone. More than 4000 **species** of trees live here, some over 50 metres (164 feet) high. Over 500 species of chattering birds search for fruit and nuts to eat. There are brightly coloured toucans, macaws and parrots, and shimmering hummingbirds searching for flowers. Many species of monkey also live here, from the tiny squirrel monkey to the large howler monkey. Boa constrictors and emerald boas slide along tree branches, alert for frogs and lizards to eat.

On the forest floor, **predators** hunt in the shadows while huge **colonies** of army ants march across the ground looking for food. Every year the Amazon river floods across much of the forest, forming the largest river basin in the world. Thousands of freshwater fish swim here, including sharp-toothed piranhas.

The African rainforest

The belt of rainforest that stretches across central Africa is the second largest rainforest in the world. It is home to an extraordinary variety of animals. Elephants, gorillas and chimpanzees live at or near ground level. Leopards hunt here too. Up in the trees colobus monkeys leap from branch to branch, while hornbills and parrots search for insects and fruit. The crowned eagle hunts up in the **canopy**.

The colobus monkey eats 2–3 kilograms (4.5–6 pounds) of leaves every day. This is about one quarter of its body weight, so the colubus has to spend about a third of its day eating.

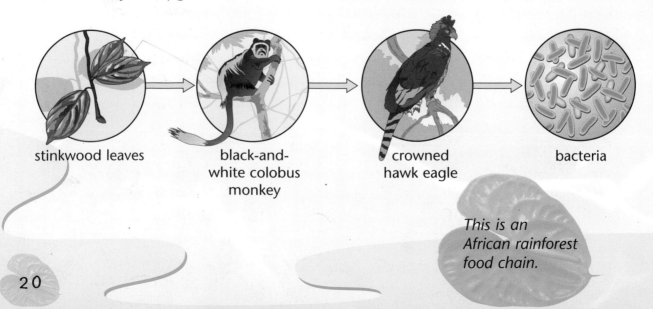

stinkwood leaves

black-and-white colobus monkey

crowned hawk eagle

bacteria

This is an African rainforest food chain.

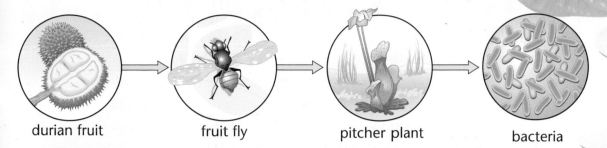

durian fruit   fruit fly   pitcher plant   bacteria

The southeastern Asia rainforest

The rainforests of southeastern Asia occur in patches, unlike the Amazon rainforest which is one continuous block. They are found in countries like Malaysia and islands such as Borneo and Sumatra. Borneo is one of the few places in the region where there are still large areas of rainforest, unspoilt by **development**, farming and wars.

Rainforest trees reach up towards the sunlight, surrounded by lianas and covered by other **epiphytes**. The forests support a huge variety of plants and animals. Many of the insects are big and brightly coloured. The stink bug and the atlas moth live among the leaves of the trees. Inside the Malaysian epiphyte *Myrmecodia* ants live as lodgers. The ants are sheltered, and in return they protect the plant from plant-eating insects. Durian trees here produce some of the smelliest fruits in the world, and brightly coloured **fungi** grow throughout the forests.

Pitcher plants are among the **carnivorous** plants of the Southeast Asian rainforest. Their leaves are shaped like a cup, with **nectar** along the rim. Insects are attracted by the nectar then fall into the cup, where they are digested by the plant.

What happens to a food web when a food chain breaks down?

All around the world, rainforest food chains and webs are under threat because of humans. Although much work is under way to stop further damage, many dangers currently face plants and animals in rainforest **habitats**.

Habitat destruction

Rainforests once covered 14 per cent of the Earth's land surface; they now cover only 6 per cent. In less than 50 years, more than half of the world's rainforests have been destroyed and the rate of destruction is increasing. Over 80,000 hectares (200,000 acres) of rainforest are destroyed every day, as trees are cut down for fuel, timber and to provide land for cattle to graze on. This **logging** is destroying the habitat for wildlife. Animal numbers are decreasing as there is less cover for **prey** to hide from **predators** and hunters. Animals are being driven further into the rainforest, to find new homes.

Scientists estimate that at this rate the last remaining rainforests could be destroyed in less than 40 years. Scientists also estimate that about 130 **species** of plants, animals and insects are becoming **extinct** every single day, often before scientists have even studied them.

Pollution

The Amazon rainforest is also at risk of **pollution** from **mining**. Brazil is rich in metals and there are many mining operations underway in the country. However, some of the chemicals from mining, such as gold, nickel and copper, run into rivers and streams in the region and are carried hundreds of miles. This pollution poisons plants and animals on and near the river, or drives them away from their natural habitat.

Overhunting

Many rainforest animals are at risk from overfishing and overhunting. In the central African rainforest, the western lowland gorilla and the chimpanzee are **endangered** animals. Both are threatened by hunting and by the destruction of their habitat. Unless they are protected they will be gone for ever.

In the central African rainforest, the male silverback gorilla is the leading member of his group.

Global warming

Rainforests have been called the lungs of the planet. This is because trees in the rainforest release the gas oxygen, which we need to breathe, into the air. They also take in large amounts of the gas **carbon dioxide** from the air during **photosynthesis**. This helps to remove some of the carbon dioxide that humans produce by burning oil and coal. When the forest is cut down, there are fewer trees to **absorb** carbon dioxide. This could make the Earth hotter and cause great damage to all living things.

Breaking the chain: how we are affected

When animals and plants are poisoned, killed or driven out of their natural habitat, it creates breaks in food chains and affects the entire food web of the region. Ultimately, breaks or changes to food chains and webs affect humans. We too can be affected by pollution and mercury poisoning. We feel the Earth heating up as rainforests that are vital for maintaining temperature are cut down. Humans along the Amazon River have fewer fish to eat as catches are reduced. Protection and management of rainforest food webs is important for all living things.

How can we protect rainforest food chains?

All around the world, scientists, **environmental** groups and governments are working to protect rainforests and rainforest food chains. They want to be sure that no further damage is done to these **habitats** and the animals and plants that depend on them.

International research and protection

Scientists and **conservationists** conduct surveys into rainforest habitats. They monitor animal and plant life in the rainforests to check that their numbers do not fall. In this way scientists find the links in the food web that need protection.

Conservation workers will study this komodo dragon at their research centre.

Scientists suggest ways for governments to improve and protect rainforest habitats, while still making the money they need out of them. Environmental groups, like Friends of the Earth, Greenpeace and WWF, **campaign** to make governments look after rainforests and to make sure people know when problems arise. They try to stop illegal **logging** and suggest other ways to manage forests.

In the Amazon, scientists, plant collectors, drug companies and conservationists are working on research into plants. They want to prove that plants within the rainforest can be used for making important drugs and cures, and could therefore make more money for countries with rainforests than chopping down the forests.

Conservation groups also run projects to teach people living in or near rainforests about how they can help to protect them, now and in the future.

Environmental groups are working hard to help conserve the world's rainforests. Fifteen per cent of the Amazon rainforest is threatened with logging like this.

Research a forest food web in your local area

You can research forest habitats in your local area, even though they are not exactly the same as a rainforest. If you go on a trip to a forest, think about the food chains of that habitat. Here are some suggestions to help you find out about animal and plant life and some tips to help you protect the environment.

1. What is the habitat like? Is it cold, warm, shady, light? How is it different from a rainforest?
2. Which plants and animals live there? Try to group them – which are the plants, insects, birds and **mammals**?
3. What do you think each animal would like to eat?
4. Which are the **predators** and which are the **prey**?
5. Can you make a food chain of the animals and plants you see?
6. Think about how the habitat could change – how would change affect the wildlife there?

Thousands of plants, animals and insects live in forest habitats, living on or near the forest trees.

27

Where are the world's main rainforests?

This map shows the location of the major rainforests of the world.

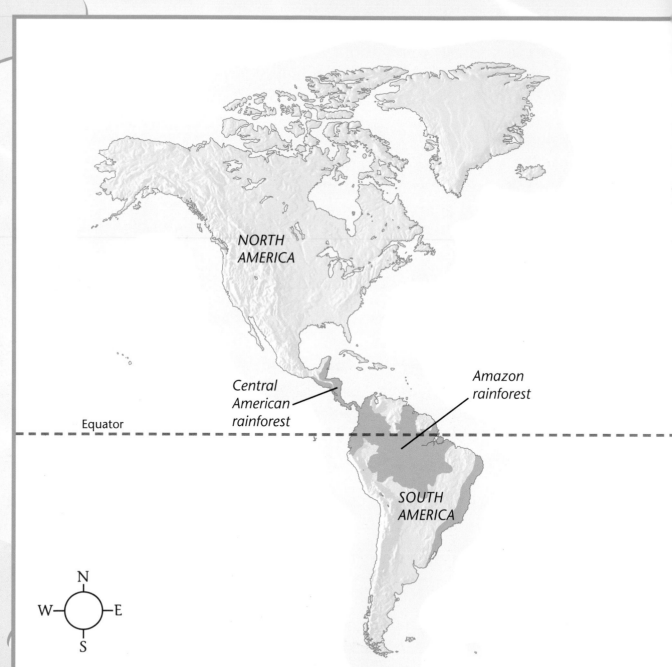

NORTH
AMERICA

Central
American
rainforest

Amazon
rainforest

Equator

SOUTH
AMERICA

N
W — E
S

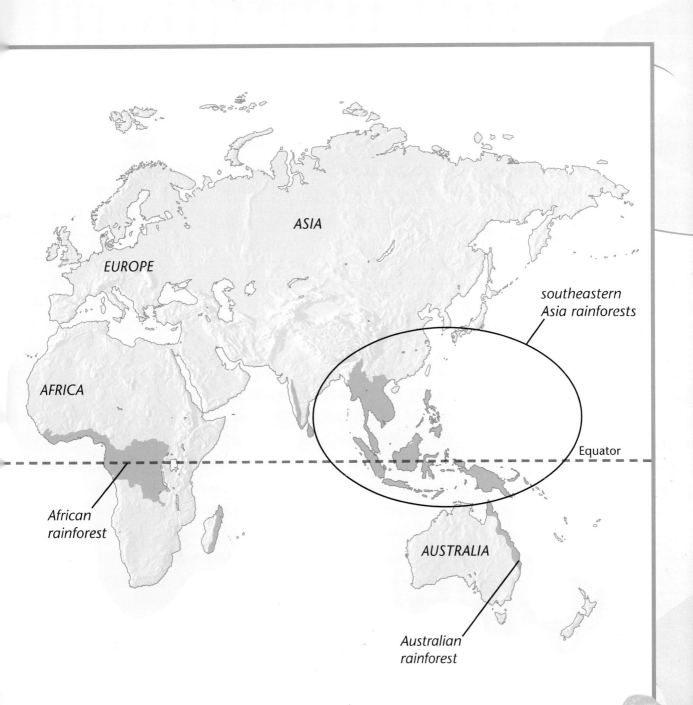

ASIA

EUROPE

southeastern
Asia rainforests

AFRICA

Equator

African
rainforest

AUSTRALIA

Australian
rainforest

Glossary

absorb take in through the surface of skin, leaves or roots

adapt change in order to survive better in a particular place

bacteria (singular bacterium) tiny living decomposers found everywhere

campaign work to get something done or changed

canopy layer of trees near the top of the rainforest

carbon dioxide gas in the air which animals breathe out and plants use to make food

carnivore animal that eats the flesh of another animal

climate the general conditions of weather in any area

colony group of plants or animals, such as insects, living together

conservation protecting and saving the natural environment

decomposers organisms that break down and get nutrients from dead plants and animals and their waste

development clearing land to put up new buildings

endangered when a species of animal or plant is in danger of dying out completely

energy power to grow, move and do things

environment the surroundings in which an animal or plant lives, including the other animals and plants that live there

epiphyte plant which grows above the ground, using other plants or objects for support, without harming them

equator imaginary line around the Earth, equally distant from the north and south poles

extinct when a species has died out completely

fungi group of decomposer organisms including mushrooms, toadstools and their relatives

habitat place where an organism lives

herbivore animal that eats plants

humidity the amount of moisture in the air

leaf litter layer of dead and rotting leaves that builds up on the forest floor

logging chopping down trees

mammals group of animals that feed their babies on milk from their own bodies

micro-organism tiny organism that can only be seen through a microscope

mining digging into the earth to find things like metal or coal

nectar sugary substance made by plants to attract insects, which eat it

nocturnal active at night

nutrients substances that plants and animals need to live

omnivore animal that eats both plants and other animals

organism living thing

photosynthesis process by which plants make their own food from carbon dioxide, water and sunlight

pollen small grains that are the male parts of a flower. Pollen combines with eggs (female flower parts) to form seeds

pollinate to take pollen from the male part of a flower to a female part

pollution when chemicals or other substances that can damage animal or plant life escape into water, air or soil

predator animal that hunts and eats other animals

prey animals that are caught and eaten by predators

primary consumer animal that eats plants

producer organism (plant) that can make its own food

rodent mammal with large gnawing front teeth, such as a mouse or rat

scavenger organism that feeds on dead plant and animal material and waste

secondary consumer animal that eats primary consumers and other secondary consumers

species group of organisms that are similar to each other and can breed together to produce young

tropical having a warm climate all year round and one or more rainy seasons

understorey dark part of the rainforest, above the forest floor but below the canopy, where only plants that do not need much light can grow

Find out more

Books and CD-Roms

Cycles in Nature: Food Chains, Theresa Greenaway (Hodder Wayland/Raintree Steck-Vaughn, 2001)

Science Answers: Food Chains and Webs, Louise and Richard Spilsbury (Heinemann Library, 2004)

Taking Action: WWF, Louise Spilsbury (Heinemann Library, 2000)

Food Chains and Webs CD-ROM (Heinemann Library, 2004) has supporting interactive activities and video clips.

Websites

www.wwf.org.uk
Find out more about conservation work at the WWF-UK website
www.wcs-congo.org
At this site you can find out all about the rainforests of Central Africa.
www.rainforest-australia.com
There is lots of information on Australian rainforests here.

Index

African rainforest 20, 23
Amazon rainforest 16, 19–20, 22–3, 24, 26
animals 4, 5, 6, 7, 8, 9, 11, 13–16, 18, 19–20, 22, 23
ants 13, 20, 21
Australian rainforest 16, 19

bacteria 4, 9, 17, 18
bandicoots 16
beetles 4, 13
birds 5, 11, 12, 14, 15, 16, 19, 20
breaking the food chain 10, 12, 22–4
butterflies and moths 12, 14, 21

canopy 5, 7, 12, 14
carnivores 8, 15, 21
chimpanzees 20
climate 5, 19
colobus monkeys 20
conservation groups 26
consumers 8, 9, 13–16, 18

decomposers 9, 17–18

eagles 5, 15, 20
endangered animals 13, 23
energy 6, 7, 8
environmental groups 25, 26
epiphytes 11, 21
extinction 12, 22

fires 10
fish 20, 23, 24
food chains 5, 6–21
food webs 4, 5, 6, 10, 22
forest floor 11, 13, 15, 17
fungi 4, 9, 13, 17, 18, 21

global warming 24
gorillas 20, 23

habitat destruction 10, 12, 22, 23
herbivores 8
hummingbirds 14, 19

insects 4, 11, 12, 13, 14, 16, 18, 20, 21
jaguars 5, 14, 15
logging 22, 26

maggots 4, 9
medicines from plants 26
monkeys 5, 8, 11, 15, 19, 20
mosses and ferns 5, 11, 13, 14

nutrients 7, 9, 11, 15, 16, 17

omnivores 8, 15, 16
organisms 4, 6, 9
overhunting 23

parrots 12, 14, 19, 20
photosynthesis 7, 24
piranhas 20
pitcher plants 16, 21
plants 4, 5, 6, 7, 8, 9, 11–12, 16, 21, 26
pollution 10, 22–3, 24
predators and prey 4, 15, 16, 19, 20, 22
primary consumers 8, 9, 13–14
producers 8, 9, 11–12
protecting food chains and webs 25–6

rainforest habitats 5, 19–21
rodents 13

scavengers 9, 17, 18
secondary consumers 8, 9, 15–16, 18
sloths 5, 14, 15
snakes 16, 19
southeastern Asia rainforest 21
sunlight 7

tapirs 13, 15
termites 18, 20
toucans 14, 19
trees 4, 7, 11, 12, 18, 19, 21, 24

understorey 5, 11